Robert E. Lee

Robert E.
LEE

Marian G. Cannon

Franklin Watts
New York / Chicago / London / Sydney
A First Book

To my husband, Jim, and to Kyle,
Griffith, Tyler, Claire, and Tucker.

Map by Donald Charles
Photographs copyright ©: cover, 30, 32, 43, 55: Library of Congress; 3: © Whitney Smith,
Flag Research Center; 16, 22, 27 (both), 29 , 36, 37, 38, 51, 58: The Bettmann Archive; 7, 11,
23 (both); The Virginia Historical Society; 9, 18 (bottom): Photri, Inc.; 10 (left):
Independence National Historical Park; 2, 10 (right), 17: Washington/Custis/Lee Collection,
Washington & Lee University, Lexington, VA; 13: National Portrait Gallery, Washington,
DC/Art Resource, NY; 18 (top), 20: Arlington House, National Park Service; 21: Missouri
Historical Society; 24, 49: Culver Pictures; 25: United States Army Center for Military
History, Washington, D.C.; 28: West Point Museum, United States Military Academy, West
Point, NY; 39: National Park Service, photo by Lon Mattoon, © Time/Life Books, Inc , from
the "Civil War" series, First Blood, pp. 164-65; 44-45: National Park Service, U.S.
Department of Interior, photo by Larry Sherer; 46: Museum of the Confederacy; 56:
Appomattox Court House National Historical Park, photo by Ronald Jennings, ©1987
Time/Life Books, Inc., from the "Civil War" series, Pursuit to Appomattox, p. 147

Library of Congress Cataloging-in-Publication Data
Cannon, Marion, G.
Robert E. Lee / by Marian G. Cannon.
p. cm. — (A First book)
Includes bibliographical references (p.) and index.
Summary: A biography of the general who commanded the Confederate Army
during the Civil War.
ISBN 0-531-20120-1 (lib. bdg.)
1. Lee, Robert E. (Robert Edward), 1807-1870—Juvenile literature. 2. Generals—United
States—Biography—Juvenile literature. 3. Generals—Confederate States of America—
Biography—Juvenile literature. 4. United States. Army—Biography—Juvenile literature.
5. Confederate States of America. Army—Biography— Juvenile literature. [1. Lee, Robert E.
(Robert Edward), 1807-1870. 2. Generals. 3. Confederate States of America. Army—
Biography. 4. United States—History—Civil War, 1861-1865.] I. Title. II. Series.
E467.1.L4C28   1993   973.7'3'092—dc20
[B]   93-415   CIP   AC

Contents

Chapter One
BORN A SOUTHERNER 7

Chapter Two
THE BEGINNING OF A HAPPY MARRIAGE 16

Chapter Three
ON TO MEXICO 21

Chapter Four
A MOMENTOUS DECISION 30

Chapter Five
LEE, THE CONFEDERATE GENERAL 36

Chapter Six
THE END OF THE WAR BETWEEN THE STATES 51

FOR FURTHER READING 60

INDEX 61

I **wish to thank** the Reader's Services Department at the Huntington Library in San Marino, California, my editor, E. Russell Primm III, and my Monday Writers Group for their advice and assistance in researching and writing this book.

Chapter One

BORN A SOUTHERNER

IN 1861, SHORTLY AFTER the Civil War began, Robert E. Lee received a message from Washington President Abraham Lincoln wanted him to command the Union army against the Confederate forces. This was a great honor for Lee. He had spent all of his adult life as an officer in the United States army and to become a general had been his dream. But Robert E. Lee refused Lincoln's offer because of his loyalty to his family and to the state of Virginia. He resigned his army commission, returned home, and later became supreme commander of the Confederate forces. To know why Lee made this decision will help to understand this famous man.

Robert Edward Lee was born in 1807 on a large plantation called Stratford Hall on the banks of the Potomac River. His family was famous throughout Virginia, mainly because his father, General Henry "Light-Horse Harry" Lee, had been a hero in George Washington's army during the American Revolutionary War and served in the U.S. House of Representatives. When General Washington died, General Lee wrote the famous eulogy describing Washington as "first in war, first in peace, and first in the hearts of his countrymen."

Robert's mother, Ann Carter Lee, also came from a well-known Virginia family. They owned the Shirley Plantation on the James River. Robert had two older brothers and two sisters.

As a little boy, Robert often rode on a horse with his father around the grounds of Stratford Hall. General Lee pointed out the different crops of vegetables and tobacco. Sometimes they visited the servants' quarters or the river pier where supply boats docked.

Robert enjoyed playing with his older brothers, Carter and Smith, and his sister, Ann, in the Lee's rambling home. Their favorite game was playing hide and seek in the many rooms and large fireplaces in the big house.

When Robert was three years old, his father lost most of his money in bad investments. He was put in debtor's prison, a place where people who owed money were sent. He was later released but the family had to move to a small

**Robert E. Lee's birthplace, Stratford Hall,
Virginia**

**General Henry Lee and Ann Carter Lee,
Robert's parents**

**The house in Alexandria,
Virginia, where Robert grew up**

house in Alexandria, Virginia, because Stratford Hall plantation now belonged to other family members.

When Robert was six years old a tragedy struck the family. The War of 1812 had begun between England and the United States. General Lee was opposed to the war, and when it was discovered that he assisted antiwar causes, he was attacked by an unruly mob. He was seriously injured and to regain his health, he went to the Island of Barbados.

Robert and his family watched from the dock in Alexandria as his father boarded the ship for Barbados. As he waved good-bye, Robert wondered if he would see his father again, but he never did. Years later General Lee died while returning home.

Mrs. Lee raised her family as best she could after General Lee left. She always encouraged her children to read and study, and their home contained a library with a large variety of books. She was also very religious. Robert and his brothers and sisters attended Christ Church in Alexandria with her every Sunday.

By age ten, Robert had grown to be a tall, handsome boy with dark hair and brown eyes. He often spent several months at a time visiting his cousins at Shirley plantation where he attended a small school the Carters operated for their own children. He later went to a public school in Alexandria. He enjoyed studying and received good grades in every subject, especially in math.

For recreation, he loved to ride one of the two family horses along the banks of the Potomac and down the streets of Alexandria, where, forty years before, George Washington had trained his troops in the town square. He liked to go to the harbor and watch as ships from foreign countries docked. In the summer, his favorite sports were running foot races with his friends and swimming in the Potomac.

When Robert was about thirteen his mother fell ill. Carter had left for Harvard University to study law, and

Smith had joined the navy. Because Robert was the only son at home, it was his job to manage the household for his mother and two sisters.

After Robert graduated from the Alexandria Academy, he wanted to go away to college, but his mother did not have enough money to send him. Robert soon formed a plan. He decided to apply to the United States Military Academy at West Point. He had always wanted to be a soldier like his father, and he also realized that he would not have to pay tuition to attend.

To go there, Robert would have to be appointed by either a U.S. Senator or Representative. When he discussed this with members of his family, a cousin, William H. Fitzhugh, said he knew John C. Calhoun, a former senator

John C. Calhoun, Lee's sponsor at West Point, the United States Military Academy

from South Carolina, who was then Secretary of War. Mr. Calhoun apparently liked to sponsor young men whose fathers had been famous soldiers, so he wrote a letter of recommendation for Robert and obtained letters from other Congressmen.

In June 1825, Robert was admitted to the Academy. When it was time to leave, he said good-bye to his mother and sisters and took a stage coach to New York City. From there, a steamer took him up the Hudson River to West Point. After landing, Robert climbed the steep river bank to the Academy. There, he saw Storm King Mountain to the north and the river far below. He realized the academy would be his home for the next four years.

At the Academy, Robert and the other cadets had to get up at five in the morning to march in formation; these were known as drills. He then attended classes and studied nine to ten hours every day. West Point's motto is "Duty, Honor, Country." Robert learned to live by these words.

He soon adjusted to the vigorous discipline and studied hard. He wanted his mother to be proud of him, because he knew it was hard on her for him to be away from home. He also wanted to follow in his father's footsteps as an army officer.

While at West Point, he tried hard not to get in any trouble. On Saturday nights, his friends often went to the North Tavern and drank ale, which was against Academy rules, but Robert never joined them. Some of his classmates thought him prudish and called him the "Marble Model." This nickname annoyed him, because he never considered himself better than the other cadets. Robert made two good friends in college, Jack Mackay and Joe Johnston, both from the South. These men later played important roles in his life.

After four years, Robert graduated second highest in his class of forty-six cadets and without a single demerit. At graduation, he was appointed to the Engineer Corps, the most prestigious group in the army. After he was commissioned a second lieutenant, he realized that all of his hard work had paid off. Now he wondered where he would be sent on his first tour of duty.

Chapter Two

THE BEGINNING OF A HAPPY MARRIAGE

BEFORE HIS FIRST assignment, Robert went back to Virginia on a short leave. He was shocked to find his mother very ill; she died a few days after he returned. In some ways, be blamed himself for her illness, because he was away so much during his years at West Point.

The month after she died, Robert was sent to Cockspur Island, Georgia, to help build a new fort, Fort Pulaski. The island was in a swampy mosquito ridden area. Lee's job was to supervise the building of drainage ditches. He was unhappy with this assignment, but realized he was in the army and had no choice as to where he would be sent.

The project at Cockspur Island was eventually abandoned, and Robert was assigned to Fort Monroe, Virginia, then under construction.

A tall, handsome man with dark hair and brown eyes, Lee was twenty-four years old when he returned to Virginia. Because he had little to do in his spare time, he decided to visit some of his relatives. He met a distant cousin, Mary Anne Randolph Custis, whom he had known

Army Lieutenant Robert E. Lee, 1838

Left, Robert E. Lee's wife, Mary Custis. Bottom, Arlington House where Mary and Robert were married.

as a child but had not seen for many years. Now that she had grown up, Robert found her very pretty. She had long blondish hair, large brown eyes, and a bubbling personality.

Mary came from a famous family and lived in a large mansion in Arlington, Virginia. She was the great-granddaughter of Martha Washington. Her father was Martha's grandson and had been adopted by George Washington.

Lee began calling on Mary at her huge home in Arlington. This mansion, surrounded by green woods, was located on top of a hill near the Potomac River. From the front of the estate, there was a wonderful view of Washington City.

After several months of courting Mary, Robert realized he had fallen in love with her. One day he arrived at her home as she and her mother were reading a novel by Sir Walter Scott. Mrs. Lee asked Robert to read for a while. Later, Mrs. Lee told Mary to bring Robert some lunch. He followed Mary out of the room and decided that this was the time to ask her to marry him. After proposing, Robert wondered why Mary was so slow in giving him her answer. She later said that she was so busy planning the wedding she almost forgot to reply.

Robert was thrilled when she finally accepted. Mary's mother very much approved of him, but her father wasn't especially happy. He thought Mary should marry someone with more money, and definitely not an army officer. Nevertheless, Mr. Custis finally gave his consent.

**Parlor at Arlington House where
Mary and Robert were married**

Mary and Robert decided to be married in the Custis' Arlington home. A large wedding was planned with six brides maids and six of Robert's friends as ushers. His brother, Smith, was his best man.

On the wedding day, because of the pouring rain, the minister arrived several hours late and soaking wet. He had to borrow a suit from Mr. Custis before the wedding could proceed. After the long delay, the minister performed the ceremony, and later everybody danced and enjoyed a festive reception. Robert was very much in love with Mary, and hoped they would have a long and happy life together.

ON MAY 13, 1846, the Mexican War began. Lee was sure he would participate in this conflict, because he had been in the army for seventeen years and had never been in combat.

By then Lee had gained extensive experience as an army engineer. After his marriage, Lee and Mary moved to Fort Monroe, where he was an engineer on the construction of the fort. The Lees' first of seven children was born there. They named him after Mary's father, George Washington Custis Lee, but everyone called him Custis.

After several other assignments, Lee traveled to St. Louis, Missouri, in 1837, as an engineer on a project to change the shifting course of the Mississippi River. At that time, people in the eastern United States considered St. Louis part of the far west and a dangerous place to live. Lee felt that this new assignment would be an adventure.

He went alone on his first trip to St. Louis. Later, he returned to Arlington, and on the second trip brought his family with him. He now had a daughter, Mary, and a son, William Fitzhugh, called Rooney. Lee and his family lived in St. Louis for three years.

The Lee family then moved to Fort Hamilton, New York. As an engineer, Lee made various changes in the for-

Robert E. Lee and son, William Fitzhugh, "Rooney," dressed for the holidays, 1845

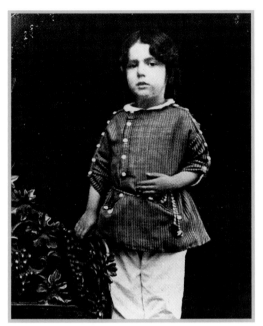

Two of Lee's seven children, Robert E. Lee, Jr., and Mildred

tifications of Fort Hamilton and other locations. The Lees lived at Fort Hamilton for five years, although Mary frequently returned to Arlington where all of the Lee's six youngest children were born. In those days, children were usually born at home, instead of in hospitals. The Lee's children included three boys and four girls.

Lee dearly loved his children and was a devoted father, who loved to romp and joke with them. Although he hated to be away from home, he felt that Mary and the children were safe and well looked after at Arlington.

In 1846, the war with Mexico began in Texas over a border dispute between Mexico and the United States. After the conflict began, Lee left Fort Hamilton to report to General John Wool in San Antonio, Texas. When the United States later invaded Mexico, he sailed on a ship to Vera Cruz as an officer with General Winfield Scott's army.

At Vera Cruz and then at Cerro Gordo, Lee's job was to scout the enemy's position. This was a difficult and dangerous assignment because he had to go very close to enemy troops.

General Scott once asked Lee to cross an impossibly rough and dangerous lava bed called the Pedregal. Lee's task was to find a route on which the troops could advance. While doing this, Lee not only found a path, he discovered

**General
Winifred Scott**

**The storming of Chapultepec fortress
near Mexico City as depicted in a
painting by James Walker**

the location of the enemy forces. General Scott praised him
highly for his work on this dangerous mission. Scott considered Lee to be one of the bravest officers he had ever
known.

Later, Lee was with General Scott's army when it
invaded Mexico City. Before the battle to capture
Chapultepec fortress, Lee was ordered to scout out the ter-
rain on horse back. While doing this, he was hit by a stray

bullet. Although Lee almost fainted, he continued on his mission. When he finally returned to report to General Scott, he collapsed. Luckily, his wound was not serious. Soon after the Americans captured Chapultepec, the troops marched into Mexico City, and the war ended.

This experience in Mexico was Lee's first taste of war. At the time, he wrote his son, Custis, telling him that a battle field was a horrible and gruesome sight. Lee had tried his best to carry out many difficult assignments, believing that it was only his duty to do so. At the end of the war, to his surprise, he learned that he was considered a war hero.

During the Mexican War, Lee met many of the men who would later play important roles in the Civil War. Some of these men became generals for both the North and the South. They included Joseph E. (Joe) Johnston, his former roommate at West Point, later a Confederate general; Jefferson Davis, later president of the Confederacy; and George B. McClellan and Ulysses S. Grant, later both generals in the Union Army.

In 1848, the treaty of Guadalupe Hildago ended the Mexican War. Because of this treaty, the United States gained a great deal of land, including the present states of Arizona, New Mexico, Utah, California, Nevada, and western Colorado.

When Lee finally returned home, he was delighted to see Mary and his children. After several other assignments,

**Joseph E. Johnston,
Confederate General,
and Ulysses S. Grant,
Union General**

**Robert E. Lee,
Superintendent at West Point**

Lee's home at West Point

he went to West Point to be the superintendent of the United States Military Academy. He was somewhat reluctant because he didn't feel qualified for the position. He spent three years there, however, during which time, his son, Custis, was a cadet.

In 1855, Lee finished his tour of duty at West Point. Now he wanted to lead troops, so he requested an assignment with a cavalry unit. After his request was approved, he learned that he would be sent to Texas.

Chapter Four

A MOMENTOUS DECISION

LEE SPENT SEVERAL YEARS with the cavalry in Texas, although his family remained in Virginia. In 1857, Lee received news that his father-in-law, Mr. Custis, had died. Getting a leave of absence, he boarded a train for Arlington.

As he traveled from Texas to Virginia, he could feel the unrest in the country. A great dispute was going on between the northern and southern states. This clash was partly a result of the different ways in which people lived. Most northerners worked in businesses and factories, while most southerners lived on plantations and depended upon slave labor to produce large crops.

Many people in the North, and some southerners, thought slavery was immoral. Lee didn't approve of slavery himself, although the practice was legal in Virginia. He believed slaves should eventually be set free. The only slave he had ever owned was an elderly man he had inherited from his mother. Before the Civil War, Lee gave him his freedom.

When Lee arrived home, he was delighted to see Mary and his children, but he was distressed that Mary was now crippled with arthritis. Soon he began settling the estate and freeing the slaves as Mr. Custis had requested.

On October 16, 1859, a fanatical abolitionist named John Brown led a heavily armed band of twenty-one in a raid at Harper's Ferry, Virginia. They captured sixty leading

John Brown, leader of the raid at Harpers Ferry

Harpers Ferry, West Virginia

white citizens and held them hostage. Brown and his supporters hoped to arouse a rebellion against slavery. Robert E. Lee was called to Washington, where he received orders to end Brown's demonstration. Lee led a unit of U.S. Marines to Harpers Ferry and overpowered Brown and his men. Brown was captured, tried, and hanged, but his uprising intensified the moral split that would eventually lead to the Civil War.

Lee was then sent back to Texas with a promotion and a new assignment. Soon after he arrived there, in December 1860, South Carolina seceded, or broke away from the United States. Six other Southern States seceded, and in February 1861 Texas joined them. These states formed the Confederate States of America.

After these events, Lee received orders to report back to General Scott, his commanding officer in Washington. Scott told Lee he would soon receive a new assignment and a promotion.

In March 1861, when Abraham Lincoln became President tensions were peaking between North and South. On April 12, 1861, Fort Sumter, a U.S. fort located in the harbor of Charleston, South Carolina, was fired upon and eventually captured by Confederate soldiers. This was the spark that started the Civil War. After that, Lincoln prepared for war by calling for 75,000 volunteers to join the U.S. Army.

Lee had always been opposed to the Southern states seceding from the Union because his father and other family members had fought in the Revolutionary War to make America free. But Lee knew that if his home state of Virginia joined the Confederate States, he would have to choose between the North and the South, a decision faced by many other Americans with conflicting loyalties.

In April 1861, President Lincoln offered Lee the position of field general of the Union Army, which meant that

**U.S. Secretary of War,
Simon Cameron.**

he would fight against the Confederate forces. Because Lee had been in the army all of his adult life, this was a great honor and a big promotion. The offer tempted him, but he also knew that he could not fight against the South. He politely refused the position, saying, "I cannot raise my hand against my birthplace, my home, my children."

At this time, Lee intended to remain in the Union Army, in a position where he didn't have to fight against the Confederacy. But when Virginia joined the Confederacy, he knew what he must do. At midnight on April 19, 1861, he wrote two letters, one to Secretary of War, Simon Cameron, and another to General Scott, resigning his commission in the U.S. Army.

Lee did not intend to fight for either side, but he then received an invitation to meet with Governor John Letcher of Virginia. In Richmond, the governor asked Lee to command the military forces of Virginia. Lee accepted, thinking it was his duty to defend his homeland. At the beginning of the war, Lee was fifty-four years old and had been in the army for thirty-six years. He wondered what lay ahead and prayed the war would be brief.

Chapter Five

LEE, THE CONFEDERATE GENERAL

AFTER THE CIVIL WAR BEGAN, Lee and most Southerners felt that they had a right and duty to protect their homeland. The Confederate States were no longer part of the United States. This new country had its own president, Congress, capital, flag, currency, and even its own song, "Dixie."

After accepting Governor Letcher's offer to command the Army of Virginia, Lee moved to Richmond. His family later joined him when the Lees' Arlington home was captured by the Union and used as its army headquarters. In May 1861, President Jefferson Davis moved the Confederate capital from Montgomery, Alabama, to

**Union troops in front of
the Arlington Mansion**

Jefferson Davis, President of the Confederacy

Richmond, Virginia. Lee felt that this was a mistake, because Richmond was only about 100 miles (61 km) from Washington, the Union capital.

At this time, many Southern officers, like Lee, were resigning from the U.S. Army and switching sides to join the Army of Virginia. Lee knew some of these men—Joe Johnston, his friend from West Point, Jeb Stuart, Richard Ewell, and John Hood. Lee's three sons and a nephew also joined the Confederate Army.

This same year, the Virginia army and the Confederate army combined, and Lee was promoted to brigadier general. Forces under his command in western Virginia lost several minor battles with the North. West Virginia became a new state and joined the Union.

Some southerners were now disappointed in Lee, saying he looked too old to be a good general, since he had white hair and a gray beard.

On July 21, 1861, the South won a stunning victory in the First Battle of Bull Run (in the South, this battle is referred to as First Manassas). The South won this battle at

The First Manassas Battle

Manassas Junction when Confederate General Thomas J. "Stonewall" Jackson ordered his men to charge the Union troops and "yell like" furies. This loud shout became known as the "rebel yell" and was repeated by Confederate soldiers in virtually every subsequent battle.

The South, however, scored no major victories for nearly a year after Bull Run, and Union General George B. McClellan's troops were advancing up the Virginia peninsula between the York and James rivers, heading for Richmond. On May 31, 1862, Confederate General Joseph E. Johnston was injured at the Battle of Seven Pines, and Lee was immediately appointed commander of the Army of Northern Virginia, the main Confederate army on the East Coast. Although the Confederates lost at Seven Pines, Lee suddenly turned the South's fortunes around. His first victories came at the Seven Days' Battle (June 26–July 1), a series of gruesome battles in which Lee forced McClellan's troops to withdraw.

Lee continued to successfully defend Richmond, and with each battle, he became more popular among the public. One reason was that he treated his men with tremendous respect. Before fighting began, he always rode his gray horse, Traveller, to the front lines to encourage his soldiers, and in the course of battles, he even slept on the ground and ate the same food as his troops.

Lee also proved to be an excellent strategist. For instance, in the battle of Chancellorsville (May 1863) Lee's

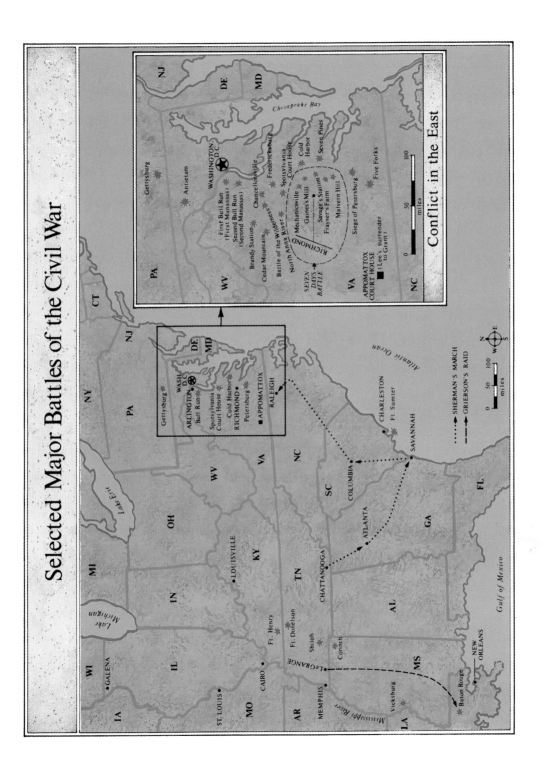

Selected Major Battles of the Civil War

Conflict in the East

Inset Map (Conflict in the East)

NJ
DE
MD
PA
WV
VA
NC

Chesapeake Bay

Gettysburg
Antietam
WASHINGTON, D.C.
First Bull Run (First Manassas)
Second Bull Run (Second Manassas)
Brandy Station
Cedar Mountain
Chancellorsville
Fredericksburg
Spotsylvania Court House
Cold Harbor
Seven Pines
Battle of the Wilderness
North Anna River
Mechanicsville
Gaines's Mill
Savage's Station
Fraysers Farm
Malvern Hill
Five Forks
RICHMOND
Siege of Petersburg
SEVEN DAYS BATTLE
APPOMATTOX COURT HOUSE
(Lee's surrender to Grant)

miles
0   50   100

Main Map

WI
GALENA
IA
MO
ST. LOUIS
CAIRO
IL
IN
MI
Lake Michigan
Lake Erie
OH
KY
LOUISVILLE
TN
CHATTANOOGA
AR
MEMPHIS
Vicksburg
LA
Baton Rouge
NEW ORLEANS
MS
LeGRANGE
Corinth
Shiloh
Ft. Donelson
Ft. Henry
AL
GA
ATLANTA
COLUMBIA
SC
CHARLESTON
Ft. Sumter
SAVANNAH
FL
Gulf of Mexico
Atlantic Ocean

NY
PA
NJ
WV
VA
NC
RALEIGH
APPOMATTOX
RICHMOND
Petersburg
Cold Harbor
Spotsylvania Court House
Bull Run
ARLINGTON
WASH. D.C.
Gettysburg
MD
DE

N
W   E
S

miles
0   50   100

······· SHERMAN'S MARCH
→ GRIERSON'S RAID

troops were outnumbered two-to-one. He divided his army and sent one division to the enemy's rear to attack encircling and surprising the enemy—a maneuver still seen as brilliant military strategy.

After each conflict, troops were moved by train to the next battle field. The soldiers fought with muskets, rifles, bayonets, and cannons, and later, with repeating rifles and Gatling guns. Covered wagons carried the supplies. At that time, the communications were still quite primitive. There were no radios, telephones, or television, and the East Coast had only a limited telegraph system.

General Lee knew that the North had far more men and supplies than the South (the Union had double the manpower of the Confederacy), so if he was to win the war, he felt he must go on the offensive. After winning the Second Battle of Bull Run (in the South, Second Manassas, August 29, 1862), Lee decided to move his troops into Maryland, a border state near Washington that sided with neither the South nor the North. His first aim was to cross the Potomac River, which he did with difficulty near the town of Sharpsburg, Maryland. He decided to make a stand and fight near the Antietam creek. Before this battle, a soldier from General McClellan's troops found a copy of Lee's secret orders in a paper wrapped around three cigars. The soldier reported this to General McClellan. When Lee learned that McClellan knew of his plans, he was very worried, and expected an early attack. But to Lee's surprise,

**The encampment of the Union Army of the
Potomac before the Second Battle of Manassas**

McClellan didn't attack until the next day, allowing Lee to reorganize his troops and double his forces.

The Battle of Antietam, on September 17, 1862, was the bloodiest single-day clash of the Civil War. Some twenty-five thousand soldiers from both the North and the South died, but neither side was a clear winner. Lee's invading forces finally became so depleted they were forced to withdraw from Maryland and returned to Virginia.

The North then received a tremendous boost, not in the battlefield, but from Washington. On September 22, five days after Antietam, President Lincoln issued the

The Battle of Antietam

Emancipation Proclamation, which stated that on January 1, 1863, all slaves in the Confederate states would be freed. At first Lee and other Southerners did not realize the impact this proclamation would have in the North and in foreign countries. After Lincoln made this declaration, France and England refused the South's requests for financial and military assistance because the Confederate states still refused to free the slaves.

**The last meeting of General Lee
and General "Stonewall" Jackson**

Lee's troops retreated from Antietam, but they were not defeated. On December 13, Lee won the battle of Fredericksburg in Virginia. After both armies spent the winter in camp, Lee scored his Chancellorsville victory (May 1–5, 1863) by dividing his troops and crushing General Joseph Hooker's forces. In this battle, Stonewall Jackson was accidentally shot by one of his own men, and died a few days later. Lee was upset, for he had lost not only a good friend, but one of his best generals.

On many fronts, the North appeared to be winning the war in 1863. Union forces had captured the city of New Orleans, and blockaded Norfolk, Virginia, and other Southern ports. On the East Coast, however, Lee's army was gaining ground. So on June 5, Lee decided he must launch a second offensive on the North. One reason Lee wanted to go North was that the South's supplies were so depleted, his troops were in danger of starving. He believed that in Maryland and Pennsylvania his troops could get food from the land to survive until autumn. The lack of food worried Lee throughout the entire war. Many times he went to Richmond and asked President Davis to send him more supplies, but none arrived.

As Lee moved into Pennsylvania, he divided his seventy thousand troops into three divisions. One division was led by General James Longstreet, who often disagreed with Lee. The others were led by Generals Richard Ewell and A.P. Hill.

On July 1, 1863, Lee arrived in the town of Gettysburg, to find that General George Meade's Army of the Potomac was already there. Lee's army under A.P. Hill came into town from the west and drove back the Northern troops. The fighting was fierce that first day, and that night, Lee met with his generals to discuss the plan of attack. They decided to strike early the next morning and recapture Big and Little Round Tops, two strategic positions held by the North. But the next day, General Longstreet didn't attack until mid-afternoon. This gave Union General Meade time to bring in additional troops, and he held the Little Round Top when the Confederates finally attacked. On the third day, Lee ordered General George Pickett's men to charge Culps Hill, a key position held by the North. "Pickett's Charge" turned disastrous. Once they were in the open and defenseless, Pickett's troops were overwhelmed by Union soldiers, and a slaughter ensued. The Battle of Gettysburg was over.

Lee was appalled that the fighting had ended so abruptly and that the South had been defeated. He was horrified at the huge casualties. Fifty-one thousand lost their lives on both sides—23,000 from the North and 28,000 from the South. Nine thousand Confederates were killed or wounded in Pickett's Charge alone. Lee lost nearly one-third of his entire army in a single battle.

Lee partially blamed himself for the Southern defeat. He wrote a letter of resignation to President Davis; Davis

**General Pickett's charge
at Gettysburg**

refused to accept it. Later, after thinking about the battle, Lee blamed General Longstreet for not carrying out his orders and attacking sooner. He said that if he had had Stonewall Jackson with him, the South would have won at Gettysburg. Some authorities say that Lee's one weakness as a general was that he was so polite some of his subordinates didn't obey his commands promptly, thinking them merely suggestions. For example, Jackson always acted on Lee's suggestions, while Longstreet did not.

These were depressing days for Lee. He had been ill earlier in the year and still felt weak. His son, Rooney, had been captured and imprisoned by a Union Cavalry unit. Rooney was in prison for almost a year. And on July 4, the day after the Gettysburg defeat, Union General Ulysses S. Grant captured Vicksburg, Mississippi, a crucial city on the Mississippi River.

The Battle of Gettysburg was the turning point of the war. After that, Lee and his troops retreated to Virginia, and the remainder of the war was fought in the Southern states. By 1864, Lee knew that the South was fighting for its life. Food supplies were low, few railroads operated, and some soldiers went barefoot and without ammunition. The North, by comparison, had more soldiers, weapons, and food.

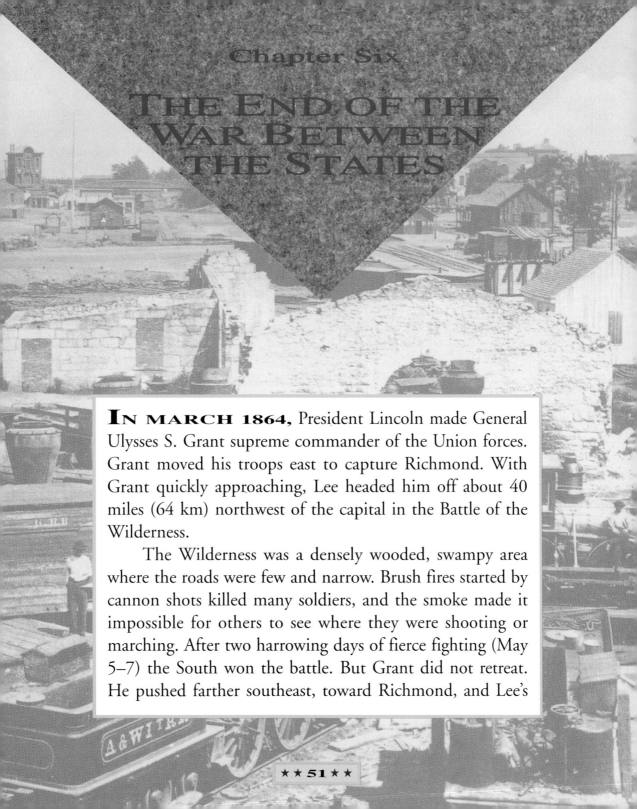

Chapter Six

THE END OF THE WAR BETWEEN THE STATES

IN MARCH 1864, President Lincoln made General Ulysses S. Grant supreme commander of the Union forces. Grant moved his troops east to capture Richmond. With Grant quickly approaching, Lee headed him off about 40 miles (64 km) northwest of the capital in the Battle of the Wilderness.

The Wilderness was a densely wooded, swampy area where the roads were few and narrow. Brush fires started by cannon shots killed many soldiers, and the smoke made it impossible for others to see where they were shooting or marching. After two harrowing days of fierce fighting (May 5–7) the South won the battle. But Grant did not retreat. He pushed farther southeast, toward Richmond, and Lee's forces hurried to meet him in another bloody battle at Spotsylvania Court House (May 8–19). Again the Confederates thrashed the Union, but again Grant drove southeast, confronting Lee at North Anna (May 23–26) and Cold Harbor (June 3–12). In every battle, the Union suffered twice as many casualties as the Confederates, but Grant persisted because he knew he had a vastly larger army to draw from than Lee. So the North pressed on, driving toward Richmond, and Lee knew Grant would not give up.

In the North, Lincoln was facing another election, and Lee thought that if he lost, the South might win its independence. But the South was being hit hard on every front. In Tennessee, General William Tecumseh Sherman had defeated the Army of Tennessee and marched into Georgia, leaving Atlanta in flames. Sherman then made his famous "March to the Sea," telling President Lincoln he would give him the city of Savannah as a "Christmas present," which he did.

General Lee, meanwhile, was entrenched in the siege of Petersburg, a crucial city that was the South's last line of defense of Richmond. Lee instructed his troops to build a maze of permanent trenches around the city, a strategy that worked so well that the Union forces were held off for ten months. Lee is given credit for anticipating "trench warfare," a military strategy used some fifty years later in World War I.

Petersburg trenches

The siege of Petersburg dragged on into 1865. On February 6, 1865, Lee was made commander of the entire Confederate army, however, it was now too late for him to unite the South. Union General Philip Sheridan had cut off his supplies from the Shenandoah Valley, and General Sherman had cut off his supplies from Georgia. Lee felt isolated. Most of his generals were gone—Stonewall Jackson and Jeb Stuart were dead, Longstreet was wounded, and A.P. Hill was sick. Food and supplies were dangerously low. People in Petersburg were eating pigeons and rats for food; a barrel of flour cost $1,200.

Lee's one last hope was to join forces with General Joe Johnston in North Carolina and somehow defeat Grant at Petersburg, thus preventing Grant from capturing Richmond. But by the end of March, Lee feared that he could no longer hold out at Petersburg. The final battle was fought at Five Forks, where the South was badly defeated.

Events then came to a rapid conclusion. On April 2, Lee sent President Davis a telegram telling him that his troops could no longer defend the cities of Richmond and Petersburg. The next day, Lee heard that Richmond was in flames, set by citizens before they surrendered the city to the Union army. Lee was even worried about his own family's safety.

Lee then directed the evacuation of Petersburg. When Lee and his troops retreated to the little town of Amelia Court House to regroup, Union soldiers surrounded them.

The City of Richmond in ruins

Lee knew now that the end was at hand. His army was too exhausted to keep on fighting, and his troops faced starvation. On April 7, Grant sent Lee a letter proposing that he surrender.

Lee told his officers he would rather die a thousand deaths than surrender, but he knew there was nothing else he could do. He sent a horseman galloping between the Confederate and Union lines of soldiers with a white flag of surrender.

**General Lee surrenders to
General Grant at Appomattox**

On April 9, in the parlor of the McLean farmhouse in the little town of Appomattox Court House, General Lee waited a half hour for General Grant. Lee wore a new uniform with gold braid and buttons and carried a sword. When Grant arrived he had on the uniform he had worn in battle. The men greeted each other and then sat at separate tables. Lee read the document of surrender, signed it, and the two men shook hands.

Lee was thankful that Grant's terms were not harsh. Grant ordered food rations for the Confederate soldiers and allowed them to return home and keep their horses.

Four days after the surrender, as Lee rode Traveller back to Richmond, a messenger brought him news that President Lincoln had been shot while attending a play in Washington. Then as he entered the city, he found destroyed bridges and burned out buildings.

In spite of the ruins around him, people lined the streets, waving and cheering as he rode by. Arriving home, he was relieved that his family was safe, and delighted to see Mary and his three daughters.

Later that month, General Joe Johnston surrendered his troops to General Sherman in North Carolina. Now the Civil War was over.

After the war, many of Lee's Southern friends were bitterly disappointed about their defeat. But Lee advised them to unite and restore the country and be loyal to the United States.

At the end of the war, there was a general amnesty, or forgiveness, for all Confederate soldiers who would take an oath supporting the United States. Senior officers, however, like General Lee, were not included. They had to apply directly to the president. Lee wrote President Andrew

General Lee in a portrait taken after the war

Johnson a number of times asking for a pardon. He waited for years, but never received a reply.

Lee wondered what he would now do to earn a living. He was offered several jobs and accepted the position of president of Washington College in Lexington, Virginia, 135 miles (217 km) from Richmond. Because this college had been closed during the war, Lee had a great deal to do to reopen it and rebuild the campus. The college was later renamed Washington and Lee University, and years later, Lee's son, Custis, replaced him as president.

Lee spent the rest of his life in Lexington and died there on October 12, 1870, at the age of sixty-three. His last words were, "Strike the tent," meaning take down the tent and leave. The war was over.

General Lee would have been happy to learn that the U.S. Congress granted him a pardon and restored his citizenship in July 1975, one hundred and five years after his death.

Robert E. Lee will be remembered as one of the most distinguished and respected generals in U.S. history. He tried for four long years to make his dreams for the Confederacy come true. He fought bravely and skillfully without adequate supplies against armies twice the size of his.

Beneath Lee's statue in the Hall of Fame in the United States Congress are these words, "Duty then is the sublimest word in our language. Do your duty in all things. You cannot do more. You should never wish to do less."

For Further Reading

Bentley, Bill. *Ulysses S. Grant.* New York: Franklin Watts, 1993.

Carter, Alden R. *The Civil War: American Tragedy.* New York: Franklin Watts, 1992.

Catton, Bruce. *The American Heritage Picture History of the Civil War.* New York: American Heritage Publishing Company, Inc., 1982 .

Earle, Peter. *Robert E. Lee.* New York: Saturday Review Press, 1973.

Roddy, Lee. *Robert E. Lee: Christian General and Gentleman.* Milford, Michigan: Mott Media, 1977.

Ward, Geoffrey C., with Ric Burns and Ken Burns. *The Civil War: An Illustrated History.* New York: Knopf, 1990.

Index

Alexandria (Virginia), 11, 12
Alexandria Academy, 13
Amelia Court House, 54
Appomattox Court House, 57
Arlington (Virginia), 19, 22, 23, 30, 36
Army of Northern Virginia, 40
Army of Tennessee, 52
Army of the Potomac, 48
Army of Virginia, 36, 38
Atlanta (Georgia), 52
Battle of Antietam, 42, 44–47
Battle of Gettysburg, 48–50
Battle of Seven Pines, 40
Battle of the Wilderness, 51
Big Round Top, 48
Brown, John, 31–32
Calhoun, John C., 13
Cameron, Simon, 35
Cerro Gordo (Mexico), 24
Chancellorsville, 40–42, 47
Chapultepec, 25
Civil War,
   Begins, 33
   Ends, 57
   Shooting war begins, 33
Cockspur Island (Georgia), 16

Cold Harbor, 52
Confederacy, 7, 33, 35, 36
Culps Hill, 48
Davis, Jefferson, 26, 36, 47, 48, 50, 54
Emancipation Proclamation, 45
England, 11, 45
Ewell, Richard, 38, 47
First Battle of Bull Run, 39
Fitzhugh, William H., 13
Five Forks, 54
Fort Hamilton, 22–24
Fort Monroe, 17, 21
Fort Pulaski, 16
Fort Sumter, 33
France, 45
Georgia, 52, 54
Grant, Ulysses S., 26, 50, 51, 52, 54, 55, 57
Harpers Ferry (Virginia), 31–32
Harvard University, 12
Hill, A.P., 47, 48, 54
Hood, John, 38
Hooker, Joseph, 47
Hudson River, 14

Jackson, Thomas J., 40, 50, 54
James River, 40
Johnson, Andrew, 58, 59
Johnston, Joseph E. (Joe), 15,
    26, 38, 40, 54, 57
Lee, Ann (sister), 8
Lee, Ann Carter, 8, 12, 16
Lee, Carter, 8, 12
Lee, Custis, 26, 29, 59
Lee, George Washington
    Custis, 21
Lee, Henry, 8
Lee, Mary, 22
Lee, Mary Anne Randolph
    Custis, 17, 19, 23, 26, 31, 57
Lee, Robert E.
    Admitted to U.S. Military
        Academy, 14
    and his children, 21, 23, 26,
        31, 57
    Appearance, 12, 17, 39
    Asked to command Union
        Army, 7, 33
    Asks for amnesty, 58, 59
    Born, 8
    Bravery, 25
    Childhood, 8, 12, 13
    Commands Confederate
        Army, 7, 35
    Dies, 59
    Education, 12

Favorite sports, 12
Graduated from U.S.
    Military Academy, 15
Marries, 19
President of Washington
    College, 59
Promoted to brigadier
    general, 39
Resigns U.S. Army, 7, 35
Superintendant at U.S.
    Military Academy, 29
Surrenders to Grant, 55
Lee, Smith, 8, 13, 20
Lee, William Fitzhugh
    "Rooney," 22, 50
Letcher, John, 35
Lexington (Virginia), 59
Lincoln, Abraham, 7, 33, 44,
    51, 52, 57
Little Round Top, 48
Longstreet, James, 47, 48, 50, 54
Mackay, Jack, 15
Manassas Junction, 40
March to the Sea, 52
Maryland, 42, 44, 47
McClellan, George B., 26, 40,
    42, 44
Meade, George, 48
Mexican War, 21, 24, 26
Mexico City (Mexico), 25
Mississippi River, 22, 50

Montgomery (Alabama), 36
Nevada, 26
New Mexico, 26
New Orleans (Louisiana), 47
New York (New York), 14
Norfolk (Virginia), 47
North Anna, 52
North Carolina, 54, 57
Pedregal, 24
Petersburg (Virginia), 52, 54
Pickett, George, 48
Pickett's Charge, 48
Potomac River, 8, 12, 19, 42
Revolutionary War, 8, 33
Richmond (Virginia), 35, 36,
    38, 40, 47, 51, 52, 54, 57
San Antonio (Texas), 24
Savannah (Georgia), 52
Scott, Winfield, 24, 33, 35
Second Battle of Bull Run, 42
Seven Days' Battle, 40
Sharpsburg (Maryland), 42
Shenandoah Valley, 54
Sheridan, Philip, 54
Sherman, William Tecumseh,
    52, 54, 57
Shirley Plantation, 8, 12
Siege of Petersburg, 54
Slavery, 31, 45
Spotsylvania Court House, 52
St. Louis (Missouri), 21

Storm King Mountain, 14
Stratford Hall, 8, 11
Stuart, Jeb, 38, 54
Texas, 24, 29, 30, 33
Traveller, 40, 57
Treaty of Guadalupe Hildago,
    26
Trench warfare, 52
U.S. Congress, 59
U.S. Engineer Corps, 15
U.S. House of Representatives, 8
U.S. Military Academy, 13–14,
    16, 26, 29, 38
Union Army, 26, 33, 35
Vera Cruz (Mexico), 24
Vicksburg (Mississippi), 50
Virginia, 7, 16, 17, 33, 35, 44
War of 1812, 11
Washington, 7, 19, 32, 33, 38,
    42, 44
Washington, George, 8, 12, 19
Washington, Martha, 19
Washington and Lee University,
    59
Washington College, 59
West Point. See U.S. Military
    Academy.
West Virginia, 39
Wool, John, 24
World War I, 52
York River, 40

About the Author

MARIAN G. CANNON is a graduate of the University of Southern California, with a major in International Relations. After college, she was part of the staff working on Cordell Hull's memoirs in Washington, D.C., and later on the staff of the League of California Cities in Los Angeles.

She has written many travel and historical articles for various national magazines and newspapers. In 1990, her book, *Dwight David Eisenhower: War Hero and President,* was published by Franklin Watts. She and her husband, Jim, live in La Canada, California. They have two adult children and five young grandchildren.

★ ★ **64** ★ ★